Triggered
II

Church Girl Problems

Experiences that shaped me, that have nothing to do with Jesus

Table of Contents

Prologue

Before y'all get all up in arms, please note, the experiences discussed in this book aren't mine alone. I have close friends who have shared their experiences and gave me permission to anonymously share in this book. I've also been an eyewitness to others' experiences. Rest assured that I am not dropping any names………… for now… JUST KIDDING!

CHAPTER 1

My Observation

Let me give you a quick summary of my history. I have been in church my ENTIRE life and I mean my ENTIRE life. Not only have I been in church, but I am also a PK (pastor's kid). I was all up and through church. I've had my hand in just about everything: singing in the choir, the praise team, playing the drums, teaching Sunday school to the youth. (Sidenote: why is it that most preachers' kids end up teaching the youth?!), junior usher board, you name it! I have been a part of MANY churches from a child to an adult; many denominations from Baptist to A.M.E, to non-denominational. I have served in administration, leadership, and even worked in "high-level" ministry positions. All I am saying is, I KNOW church; from the scriptures to the traditions, to the organizational side, ALL OF IT!

I have seen the good, the bad, and the ugliness of church. There are many things I've been taught, that to be honest, I didn't understand. I listened and watched a lot of things transpire that really didn't line up with the Word of God (Bible). I mean, that's what we are supposed to live by right? Where did these "rules and regulations" come from? By-Laws? Why did it seem that different denominations had different interpretations of the Bible? It's the SAME BIBLE (at least I thought)! I had so many questions! The kicker to all of this was, I couldn't find the answers to these questions because technically speaking, I shouldn't be asking them. It's like this unspoken rule. You don't question the pastors, deacons, ministers, or any other leader really. I feel like the expectation is to blindly follow whoever's interpretation of the Word regardless of if it makes sense or not. Altogether, it was super weird.

The purpose of this book is not to BASH the church. I love God and His church. But my goodness His PEOPLE though?! That's a whole 'nother story. My hope is to shed some light on ideologies we've grown up thinking are good or true and things that have been ignored or swept under the rug. I believe we need to merge our human nature and experience with our spiritual nature. Yes, the "spirit man" is supposed to be the strongest in our lives. We all know that what we nurture grows; you know we are supposed to die to our flesh. The Bible says, “And those who belong to Christ Jesus have crucified the flesh with its passions and desires”. (Galatians 5:24 ESV) Dying to it shouldn’t mean ignoring it though. Things just don’t go away if you ignore it. Yes, the devil will flee when we resist. “Submit yourselves, then, to God. Resist the devil, and he will flee from you.” (James 4:7 NIV) But I don’t think “resist” and “ignore” are synonymous. After all, you can't “resist” what you don’t acknowledge is there. Uh oh.

Truth is, I’ve experienced A LOT of hurt in the church; it’s one of the places I loved the most. In that same notion, I was severely hurt by people that I THOUGHT were supposed to love me unconditionally. A lot of principles and values I learned came from the church and some of them were just flat out wrong. Some things I was taught to believe turned out to not be true after all. For instance, at times it felt like we were supposed to be superhuman. I understand we aren't supposed to sin. We are supposed to resist temptation. But HOW?! What am I supposed to do with these feelings? I prayed SEVERAL times, but I was still struggling. Some things happened to me that deeply affected me. I prayed AGAIN. But I still dealt with the residue of trauma. Am I not "Christian" enough? I am obviously not doing something right. Bad things keep happening to me, even when I am trying my best to do things right. I was told to serve more, and I did. They also told me that since things are going wrong; it MUST be because I'm not praying, reading, or fasting enough (it couldn't possibly be God taking me through a season to stretch and prepare me for His purpose) But yet again, here I am still on the struggle bus.

It wasn't until I decided to take a major step back from what I knew to be normal to be able to see things differently. Something just wasn't right. I've matured in my walk with God, and there are some things that I know for myself. I see that I have lived in this spiritual fantasy where I was made to believe things that weren't real or true. It bothers me that currently most of what I see in churches still operates this way. In John 8:32 (ERV) it says, "You will know the truth, and the truth will make you free." What truth are we talking about here? The Word of God is truth. We believe it, we quote it, and try our best to live it out. BUT there's a missing piece we overlook or ignore. We are HUMAN. Yes, we are saved, sanctified, fire baptized, and filled with the Holy Spirit; AND we also experience trauma that negatively affects how we think, feel, and show up in the world. Both statements are in fact TRUE; AND I believe ignoring the latter statement is the cause of why most of us that are Christians struggle so terribly. We have these spiritual gifts that are needed to help build the Kingdom, but our character doesn't quite match the calling. Our character is our inner being that was built over our lifetime from our experiences, whether those experiences be good or bad. Perhaps this is why there are so many fallen preachers. The preacher knows the word of God, they're charismatic, etc. But every time you turn around there's a scandal with him sleeping with everyone other than his wife. How can these things co-exist? He must be a hypocrite, right? The devil? Maybe. Or he never addressed the fact that he was molested and exposed to porn at a young age. Uh-oh. We don't talk about that though. There are statistics at our fingertips that tell us how sexual abuse negatively affects children psychologically and physically. Therapy is typically needed for individuals to overcome the effects of this abuse in hopes not to be a victim again or become the abuser. But in the church, for some odd reason, we don't feel this step is necessary. We will pray about it, and then not talk about it anymore. Maybe in our minds we think "if we pray about it, it will go away or", or the consequences of trauma are blocked by the prayer. It's 2024. This has not or ever will be the case. In James 2:14-24, it talks about faith and good works. It literally says if we have faith and do nothing the faith is worth nothing, or “faith without works is dead.” “Works” is not just some random action. Those actions or “works” should line up with what we are declaring we are believing for. It gave the example in the 15th and 16th verse, if someone comes to you in need of clothes or something to eat, and you say, “aye man praying for you I hope you get what you need”, you’ve done absolutely nothing. If this is the Word of God, then why do we avoid therapy? Why do we avoid acknowledging out loud the things that have happened to us and we’re struggling? Why do we avoid doing the inner work for us to heal? We would rather make up these ideologies that have nothing to do with Jesus and the Word of God.

SIDENOTE: ***Speaking of Jesus, He literally went through a HUMAN experience. He felt pain, hunger, anger, etc. and ACKNOWLEDGED it. The difference is He didn't sin. Unfortunately for us, He is the only perfect one. We WILL sin, He told us that. Romans 3:23 says we ALL have sinned and fallen short. If He acknowledges His human experience. Why do we ignore ours?***

All of this and then some are the reasons this book was created. I really want my people to be healed and FLOURISH!! Enough is enough at this point. We must start having these uncomfortable conversations, addressing what's been swept under the rug, and tear down these false church ideologies. There are people out there that really need Jesus, but we must deal with ourselves first.

Reflective Moments

What have you observed in church? How have your observations affected you?

CHAPTER 2

The Heart of the Matter

I believe one of the challenges with the body of Christ are the matters of the heart, the human part of our being.

We have created this idea that the "spirit" in which we are supposed to operate is separate from the heart, even though we know that the mind, heart, and spirit, are all connected; or they should be.

Let's look at it like this. It is true that we can operate in the gifts of the spirit (check out the gifts of the spirit in 1 Corinthians 12:1-11 not the same as FRUIT of the spirit) whenever God uses us even when our heart isn't whole; but that doesn't mean we should ignore the matters that are in our heart. It seems like we've been conditioned that way. Versus working on healing our hearts so we can be fully utilized by God and miss the least amount of what He has for us.

Ignoring heart matters eventually leads to self-destruction. Think about how many issues you've seen or heard about in the church. No, really think about it. You have ministry leaders caught in adultery (I mean will have a whole wife but bring their girlfriend to church), become ego driven, are pedophiles, have issues with porn, are thieves, etc. Or you have all this backbiting, and quarreling among members because everyone wants to feel important.

Everyone is supposed to wait til they're married to have sex, but the children's church is PACKED with babies. We talk about people who come into the church not "dressed right". Often, guilt and shame are used as tools of control even those specific things are antithetical to the Word of God. ALL of this and more is going on. Everyone sees it and feels it. BUT NO ONE WANTS TO TALK ABOUT IT OUT LOUD AND ADDRESS IT. We ignore it.

We would rather focus on the spiritual gifts. They have a gift for what they do when it comes to preaching, teaching, or prophesying the word of God. So, it gets hella confusing when it comes to the question of should I listen? Should I follow? Or what? I mean, it's no different than David, right? He was a man after

God's own heart, but MAN did he have some issues.

Or what about the other issues of the heart that we don't want to talk about, like abandonment from absent parents, emotionally immature parents, divorce, molestation, poverty, and so much more. We are deeply affected by these events in our lives (trauma), but we ignore these experiences; or create this spiritual fantasy in our minds that we will overcome or grow past these things if we just do spiritual things like slap some oil on ourselves and pray. We believe these issues, that are sometimes embedded in our DNA (we haven't even touched on generational curses), are just going to magically disappear. This has NOT been the case for anyone in the history of time from the Bible until now.

SIDENOTE: ***How much more effective could the body of Christ be if we went below the surface and healed from our heart issues? How many more people would we be able to reach if we were more transparent about things we have experienced and overcome? How much greater would our impact be if we increased our Emotional Intelligence in addition to having the Word of God?***

Reflective Moments

What are the matters of YOUR heart that have affected you?

CHAPTER 3

Indirect Message:

"Cover your body so you don't cause your brother to fall"

I find myself sitting in deep reflection about what I learned to believe about who I was as a woman, womanhood itself, and life as a Christian woman. I've sat and thought long and hard about specific things I was told directly and indirectly. I don't remember being told I was beautiful either inside or out. I can't recall a time when someone spoke life or affirmed me UNLESS I was doing something for the ministry. A lot of my peers have had the same experience. What I DID hear a lot was, "make sure that skirt isn't too tight and over your knees, make sure you have on some stockings, put on a slip, possibly put on a girdle." Now it doesn't matter if it's 12,000 degrees outside; you BET NOT come up there with no spaghetti straps. Sleeveless is pushing the envelope. Shoulders should be covered. Make sure them bosoms are strapped down good. The bottom line is to not be a distraction. You are not here to be "sexy". Be MODEST and not fast. What does "being fast" even mean? Are we not going to address the fact that some of these men (ministers, deacons, pastors) had wandering eyes?

So, instead of dealing with them and their lustful nature and lack of self-control, we are going to place responsibility SOLELY on women to NOT entice them?!?!. What kind of message does that send to your young ladies? Do you know how many times I've heard "don't be the reason a man stumbles?" Don't get me wrong here. I'm older now and totally understand appropriate attire; you know, there's a right time and place for everything. But come on now.

Unknowingly, the seed of shame and guilt and a little people pleasing was planted. It's unfair to a young girl to have to go to CHURCH and be on guard about her body or her looks in general; making us responsible for someone else's perverted nature. Most of us heard negative messaging surrounding our bodies in the CHURCH.

<u>**SIDENOTE:**</u> ***Why is the first place I hear body positivity somewhere else other than the church? Why did we think modesty and shame were synonymous?***

It felt like women were good for everything else BUT to preach in the pulpit. I distinctly remember going to churches we fellowshipped with to hear men talk about not believing in women preachers. So, imagine the negative body talk AND hearing this? Doesn't sound very empowering, does it?

All of this going on and at no point was there any affirmation. Was I kind? Was I smart? Did God have a plan and a purpose for my life too? At that point, no one has ever said that to me. That can have a negative effect on a person you know. A kid with minimum affirmations during the formative years can grow up to be an adult who tends to shrink themselves in certain spaces or have low self-esteem and constantly seek the validation of others. Honestly, I didn't know that affirmations were something I needed until I started noticing these patterns of shrinking and low self-esteem within myself. Connecting the dots has revealed A LOT!

Reflective Moments

Have you been affected by the idea of "causing your brother to fall"?

CHAPTER 4

Direct Message

"The more you serve, the more blessed you'll be"

All I knew how to do was "serve". I found that the more I served, the better I served, the more praise received. It felt good to have positive acknowledgement. (I go on later and found out this is a dysfunction called **people pleasing** *-a person who feels a strong urge to please others, even at their own expense.* They may feel that their wants and needs do not matter or alter their personality around others, but we will address that later). I already struggle with boundaries as it is. **(remember**

we talked about unresolved issues we never address; this was one for me) Boundaries were mostly nonexistent when it came to the church. A lot of my peers and I would take on too much responsibility, sometimes neglecting our own, stretch ourselves too thin, and eventually burnout. In most cases, burnout (per **Merriam Webster:** *an exhaustion of physical or emotional strength or motivation usually because of prolonged stress or frustration*) is a sign that something in the situation needs to change. But in church there's an implication that this shouldn't happen. Either you're in sin, or not living right in some capacity.

I was so busy doing church work, you know, my "reasonable service", that my RELATIONSHIP with God suffered. Imagine that. It was so hard to decipher His voice. I sought wisdom from leaders on this struggle. All I ever wanted to do was to do what God wanted me to do, at the right time, in the right season with the right people and wanted to make sure I had clarity. I'm not sure what advice I thought I would receive. Maybe I thought they would pray with me; we would all touch and agree together OR they would intercede on my behalf. That didn't happen. Maybe I thought they would give me a list of scriptures or prayer strategies to speak to myself. That didn't happen either. The advice I would receive would typically revolve around doing "more". Or there was some type of indirect implication that I had too many "outside" or "worldly" distractions. Sin wasn't my probably nor was being in "the world". It's interesting that no one thought "church busyness" fell into the category of "distractions", hmmm.

I subscribed to this ideology of "serving through your pain" ... This is one of the worst ideas I've had in my adult life. Think of it the same as going to work sick as a dog. I feel like some years back it was praised to "do what you have to do" or "pressing your way" because you have mouths to feed. However, post pandemic we are more conscious of others and how we can spread germs, and most importantly we realized it is way harder for our bodies to heal when it doesn't rest when it's not well. So, if we have adopted more current ideas when it comes to work life balance and health, how come we don't do the same in the church? When the test and trials of life are wearing people down, why then do we suggest "serving more" to literally take more energy than we must give. When your heart is broken it’s hard to think straight. It’s just like sickness in my opinion. Why dehumanize our experience to say, “put your issues aside and serve because someone needs you.” “No one cares what you’re going through at the moment.” “Leave your problems at the door to come serve.” Who is making sure those of us that serve don’t leave and pick it right back up? AGAIN, God literally sent Jesus to the Earth to have a HUMAN experience. He was tempted, had pain, hunger, etc. just like we’ve endured. The difference is He OVERCAME by leaning into His Father. He didn’t ignore it or just move past it.

I think about all the things I have suffered in my life and how I still served because I thought that’s what God wanted me to do. I didn't want to disappoint God. At one point in time, I was literally in an apartment with no electricity, getting dressed in the dark, getting on the bus for church because my car was down, and crying all the way just to go sing. Why? Because it was about the people, I am supposed to do this. I get to do this! They need me to serve to help usher in His presence. Again, I didn't want God to be mad at me. Is that how it works though? I think about all these moments I had **struggling and serving**. Did the leaders know? Some of them did. It would've been so helpful to have someone sit me down and ask me what was wrong and listen to me. My life probably would've turned around sooner had I had someone to walk the journey with me or connect me to someone that could help in this area or share their own experience and how they made it through. Is this what we would call "discipleship"?

SIDENOTE: ***I know what you're thinking, where on earth is the discipleship? We are talking about a church, right?***

TAKE NOTE: "Unaddressed behaviors repeat themselves"

Reflective Moments

Have you been the person who "served through your pain"?

CHAPTER 5

Direct and Indirect Messages:

"Sex……... IDK"

"If you have sex before marriage you're going to hell- but where all these babies coming from in this church"

"Purity culture"

"No prep for marriage, but the marriage bed is undefiled though"

"Sexual urges … ya nasty suppress them until marriage"

"Be a good wife- how? Cus he knows how to cook and clean for himself"

"Don't have babies out of wedlock but if you do, you'll be brought before the church can't serve til after you have the baby"

Now I am not going to dive too deep into this subject (there's so many layers to peel back with this subject). As you can see, there are quite a few direct and indirect messages dealing with this; and these aren't all of them. But let's tiptoe on the fine line of this subject, shall we? Myself, my peers, and associates have had similar experiences dealing with sex. In a nutshell, in church the conversation mostly consisted of making sure we didn't have sex before marriage because we were going to go to hell. If you sin, and just so happen to be a woman who ends up pregnant, you must then be "sat down" if you serve in ministry. You may be asking, well what about the other person fornicating, the man? Well, I'm not sure if anything happened or not. I know a few stories where the man didn't get sat down. If he served, or was a paid employee, he still was able to continue with business as usual. Maybe the men of the church did address the man, it was just in private. I can only comment based off what I see. In some cases, the pregnant woman is brought before the church to apologize and ask for forgiveness. If I could insert a pause here, I would. What about the other people that YOU KNOW are fornicating too?? Nothing. Those people just didn't get "caught". We only address the sin we can see (uh oh).

Now on the other end, we are told marriage is the solution to your burning flesh (at least that's what they told us) (yes, the Bible talks about this, but I think it was taken out of context). So, we are encouraged to marry. Goodness. Let me get this straight, all through childhood and teenage-hood, I am ashamed about my developing body, engrossed in the idea of making sure I don't "cause my brother to fall", and told if I have sex before marriage I am going to hell. NOW I'm grown. NOW "I need to find me a husband". NOW year after year I am asked why I don't have a husband. NOW I need to make sure I keep my weight down so I can "get me somebody". THEN, I "find" someone and NOW I need to make sure I "keep him happy". The marriage bed is undefiled. HOW. ON. EARTH. WOULD. I. KNOW. HOW. TO. DO. ANYTHING?!?!?!??? What does that even mean? Are we going to talk about what love is and what it is not (1 Corinthians 13)? Or does that matter? Is anyone going to explain the reality of marriage here? I remember being given advice from different extremes from different ends of the spectrum. On one hand I would say I really want to be married. I would have unhappy married people say that's not what I wanted. Then I wouldn't mention at all and try to live content. NOW my sexuality is being questioned, and I'm imposed with this thought that something was wrong with ME. I can go on and on BUT I am going to digress here.

SIDENOTE: ***Perhaps SELF CONTROL is what should've been encouraged to those who had that "burning flesh"?***

Reflective Moments

Did the church have a positive or negative influence on how you viewed sex?

CHAPTER 6

Indirect Message

"Why does turning the other cheek feel like the other person gets away without taking accountability?"

Now in Matthew 5:38-40, it talks about if someone slaps you, give them the other cheek to slap; and if someone wants to sue and take your shirt, go ahead and give them your coat too. Let's insert a side eye right here. Even though most of us feel some type of way reading this scripture, we can understand that Jesus was telling us not to take revenge when we are done wrong. Ok we got it. It appears this scripture is twisted, weaponized, and used by the offender in the situation to by-pass conflict resolution.

It's interesting to mention turning the other cheek, or extending grace in these moments, which are biblical but used in a manipulative manner. But what about Matthew 18:15-17? If you have an ought with your brother, you go to them, right? What happens when the "brother" doesn't want to listen or talk about it? What happens when the "brother" doesn't want to acknowledge their contribution to the offense? What happens when it's a leader that's the "brother"? I'm sure your chest got tight there. I have found myself in this situation quite a few times in my lifetime. Honestly, I am not sure how well I have handled things before. The best thing I knew to do after multiple attempts of "making things better" with no apology or changed behavior from the other party, I felt it was best to leave. Even with trying to leave on good terms, it turned into something else. In this one ministry position, I had one instance where I put in a 3 week notice and was fired immediately after. Then of course, I had the indirect implication not to even come back to the church. I mean were they mad or nah? I can't explain the hurt I felt in these situations. I didn't understand why people "disposed" of me completely. Technically I am the one that left. But man, just because the dynamic of the relationship changed, didn't mean we couldn't be connected at all. Right? It took me going through similar situations to realize, sometimes if people can't have full access to you, they don't want you at all. It hurt, but I had to learn how to move on. Some may ask, why did it hurt so bad if YOU left? Well, maybe I thought there still would be a relationship there. I wasn't just a volunteer or an employee of these places. I had a relationship with these folks. Can I be vulnerable? I felt like I was disposed of, you know, like thrown away. It felt like everything was all good when they had full access. If there were no boundaries between us, everyone was happy………. Except me. I thought I meant something to these folks. I thought we were like family. I set a boundary. Instead of respecting it and adjusting to it, they abandoned me. At least that's how I felt. I just couldn't understand why it was so easy for people to walk away and act like I was nothing. There was no acknowledgement of their part, no apology, no nothing. Did the fact that they hurt me even cross their mind? How was I to blame for responding to the hurt that was caused to me?

Reflective Moments

Have you been in a situation in church where conflict was handled improperly?

CHAPTER 7

Is this an IDENTITY Crisis?

As I think about my experience, I think about all the programming, all the messaging that helped shape who I have come to be, and why I'm in therapy trying to undo some of this mess. In everything that I've named so far, I can't recall too many times where I was AFFIRMED just as the person God created me to be. If I am being super transparent, some of the most hurtful things I've heard about myself have come from people in the church, even AT church at times! Power of life and death is in the tongue, right? So why was there minimal life being spoken? If guilt and shame were antithetical to Christ characteristics, then why was this the method used to "help shape people"? The Bible literally says to think on these things, "Finally, brothers and sisters, whatever is true, whatever is noble, whatever is right, whatever is pure, whatever is lovely, whatever is admirable—if anything is excellent or praiseworthy—think about such things." (Philippians 4:8). Don't get me wrong here. I believe CORRECTION and ACCOUNTABILITY is a part of love. I also believe it's not just one sided, no one is above the reproach (unless I missed a scripture saying otherwise). I believe there are better ways to do this than condemnation. The Bible tells us, "A soft answer turns away wrath, but a harsh word stirs up anger." (Proverbs 15:1 ESV) It also says, "Let your speech always be gracious, seasoned with salt, so that you may know how you ought to answer each person." (Colossians 4:6)

What's the point of all this anyway?

Let me have a super **TRANSPARENT** moment with y'all. I've discovered that I had an unhealthy attachment with church that negatively affected my relationship with God (read that again). I know, I know, that sounds weird right? It's almost like "the church was my identity". It still sounds weird, doesn't it? Here is what I've observed. It seems like the church (not all of course) was the place people came to worship God AND be somebody; somebody important. Depending on what you did, your gifts would give this sense of notoriety. You were praised! As humans, when we are praised, naturally you want to do more. It's like positive reinforcement. Most people I know grew up in homes where affirmations, positive speech, and positive self-esteem weren't necessarily a big part of the upbringing. Maybe for some people, this may be the first place you were noticed in a POSITIVE light. Someone told you "Good job", patted you on the back, and gave you a TITLE at that (now we aren't going to talk about if your character was ready for the title or not mmkay). Everywhere else in the world you're just a number. OR let's be real; you're everything else but a child of God. So of course, when you find a space where you find community and a sense of self you hold on to it for dear life. This was me in a nutshell. I found community and a sense of self in church.

Most would ask what's wrong with that? You're in church, you're serving, you feel important, it's all good right? Nah. Where in all of this have, I said that there's a "relationship with God" developing? Where in this did I say I saw people being delivered from their weights and sins? Where did I mention that I see people healed from trauma they've experienced in their lives? I didn't. I am sure this happened for some people. But for most US, we were just covering up those issues and dysfunction-ing. What I found is instead of truly depending on God, I was depending on the people of God. I mean I read the Bible, prayed and fasted. But listen more to the leaders for direction than God. Maybe in my head I thought it was one in the same. We know God uses people to give you a word or confirm things for you. Where I messed up is being strong in my relationship with God for myself to be confident in what He tells me directly. Anything else people say would confirm IF it is from Him. It took me a while to understand that. I have allowed myself to be underestimated, mishandled, overlooked, disrespected, stunted, and taken advantage of all within a place I loved dearly (and still do) and thought loved me too! How could the place that's supposed to be like a hospital, a place where I can find healing be the place that has caused the most pain? How could I pour so much into a place where I don't find replenishment? Well, the very short answer to that is because I didn't deal with my internal issues, such as lacking boundaries and low self-esteem, burnt-out, several times over.

So many things have been said up until this point. My hope is that you feel seen and heard through this book. I also hope that being more transparent about things we learned that really didn't have anything to do with Jesus allows you a chance to have your own epiphanies and work through some stuff.

I am deeply concerned about the way the world is going; I am concerned about my fellow believers especially. We are saved, sanctified, filled with the Holy Spirit; talented, gifted and seem to be hurting the most. We read and know the Word but seem to struggle with living the abundant life God says we can have here on Earth. We seem to be so lost in finding, knowing, and walking out our purpose. We are flawed humans saved by grace. But the human part of us gets ignored. Notice I said IGNORED. I truly believe we have this idea that when we accept salvation, somehow the Holy Spirit automatically overpowers our "carnal" or human side, and the issues we had before just magically go away; well at least we think that's how it ***should*** happen. When in the history of humanity has this worked? It HASN'T. We have lived and witnessed some of the most Holy Ghost filled men and women of God fall terribly. I am not just talking about sin either.

Some of the saints have some terrible character flaws. Oh. You're going to sit there and act like you don't know what I am talking about? Say less. Some of the saints are the most arrogant, anxious, dishonest, greedy, indecisive, narcissistic, manipulative, worrisome, self-righteous people I have encountered in my adult life. Hey but those same people will shout you out any day of the week. Is this a contradiction? Is this the reason why non-believers call believers hypocrites? Perhaps they have some knowledge of God and what he says the character of a believer should look like. What does the Bible say? I'm glad you asked! In Galatians 5:22-23 he gives some attributes called the Fruit of the Spirit. These are characteristics of a believer: love, joy, peace, forbearance, kindness, goodness, faithfulness, gentleness, and self-control. If these are supposed to be the attributes that shine the most, then why don't they? We know that spiritual gifts are given without repentance; but the poor character traits are turning people away.

In addition to not being good Christ reps on Earth, a lot of us live a life beneath God's best for us. We struggle to find and fulfill our purpose. It's hard to believe you are destined for greatness when you have a voice in your head saying otherwise. I mean if all you heard as a child "you're not going to amount to anything" and you've never addressed it, that's the voice that's the loudest a lot of times.

One of the best books I've read is "Emotionally Healthy Spirituality" by Peter Scazzero. It literally changed my life. A summary of the book is, "his primary observation is that it is impossible to be spiritually mature while remaining emotionally immature. He believes there is a link between emotional and spiritual health." (**Emotionally Healthy Spirituality, by Peter Scazzero**) I couldn't agree more! Once I read this book and took a deep dive to questions, I couldn't answer about myself; "why do I continue to end up in situations where I'm being used" "why I agree to things I don't want to do" "why I always end up being burnt out", etc. I decided to go to therapy. I'm not going to lie to y'all. I wrestled with this idea for a long time. I just didn't want to admit there was something wrong with me. Once I started therapy, I found that I was able to answer those questions. In addition to that, I started peeling back layers of things I didn't know existed. This was an ugly nasty process. BUT it wasn't until I peeled back those layers, I could put a name on those things I struggled with. This changed my conversations with God tremendously. The Bible says we should cast all our cares upon Him, right? Here's a thought I want to challenge you with. If we ignore our issues and act like they don't exist, how can we cast those things on Him? **We can't cast what we don't acknowledge exist right?**

CHAPTER 8

Conclusion

The point of sharing my thoughts with y'all is merely to say deprogramming the messages of the church isn't something to put everyone up in arms. Change in thinking can be super hard. I merely want to offer a different perspective and suggest a different way of thinking about things. I believe for us to truly walk in the purpose God gave us and to help disciple others to do the same, we are going to have to be transparent. We are going to have to have hard conversations. We may have to pivot, adapt and change what we've always done. Just because it's working doesn't mean it's effective. Just because people show up doesn’t mean people are impacted. Where there's impact there will be change. Where change is we see GROWTH. I love you!

Reflective Moment

How do you define IDENTITY in Christ? Do you know who you are?

____

____

____

____

____

____

____

____

____

____

____

____

____

____

____

FOR MORE CONTENT, CHECK OUT THE PODCAST ON YOUTUBE, CHIC LIFE NETWORK!!

https://www.youtube.com/@getchiclifenetwork

www.ingramcontent.com/pod-product-compliance
Lightning Source LLC
LaVergne TN
LVHW050542100826
845148LV00002B/652

* 9 7 8 1 7 3 4 9 7 3 2 5 9 *